SELL YOUR HOUSE

HOW TO UPSELL YOUR HOUSE IN A DOWN MARKET

RACHEL S. KRUEGER

Outskirts Press, Inc.
Denver, Colorado

The opinions expressed in this manuscript are solely the opinions of the author and do not represent the opinions or thoughts of the publisher. The author has represented and warranted full ownership and/or legal right to publish all the materials in this book.

Sell Your House
How To Upsell Your House In A Down Market
All Rights Reserved.
Copyright © 2009 Rachel S. Krueger
v2.0

Cover Photo © 2009 JupiterImages Corporation. All rights reserved - used with permission.

This book may not be reproduced, transmitted, or stored in whole or in part by any means, including graphic, electronic, or mechanical without the express written consent of the publisher except in the case of brief quotations embodied in critical articles and reviews.

Outskirts Press, Inc.
http://www.outskirtspress.com

ISBN: 978-1-4327-3728-3

Library of Congress Control Number: 2008940469

Outskirts Press and the "OP" logo are trademarks belonging to Outskirts Press, Inc.

PRINTED IN THE UNITED STATES OF AMERICA

EDITED BY: KRISTY CALDWELL

HETTIE ORANGE SMITH

AND

RACHEL KRUEGER

I dedicate this book to my mom and dad for instilling in me that I could do anything in life as long as I put my mind to it.

To my brother, Robin, for teaching me how to dream big.

To my husband, Brandon, for believing in me and making me see that I can overcome procrastination.

and

To Kristy, for being the best cheerleader anyone could ever have!

INTRODUCTION

First of all, I am thrilled you purchased this guide! You've taken the first positive step toward selling your house. My book is going to help you see that before you go to the closing, you must first "sell" your house to the prospective buyer. The real estate market can be tough sometimes, and we need to set your house apart from others. This guide is going to help you achieve that goal. You are going to sell your house by creating an environment that will convince the buyer your house is the house for them. It's going to take a little time, and a little hard work, but I have faith that if we can make it through this process with as little frustration as possible and laugh a lot along the way, you are going to get your house sold.

There are over 100 different things to look at inside and outside your home. I've designed this guide to give you low–to–no cost ways to go about addressing these issues. You may have already tackled some things on our list or ones I haven't mentioned, and if so, you're ahead of the game!

I want you to open your eyes and your mind, become the homebuyer, and really try to see your house from that perspective (as the homebuyer). This can be a hard exercise for some people, because you're so used to your surroundings, and seeing the "problems" in your home may be difficult for that reason. This is where your OP will come into play and really help you out, but we'll talk more about that later.

What I want you to understand, and this is strictly my opinion, is that most people cannot see beyond what is in front of them at that moment. For instance, say that the color of your living room is what you consider a beautiful shade of blue, but the prospective homebuyer may think just the opposite. That little tidbit could make or break the sale of your home to those people simply because their furnishings wouldn't match! Yes people, those things like paint color, the condition of your own furnishings, and much more are key in selling your home. There are many people who just simply want to move in and not have to tackle a bunch of projects right off the bat. On that note, we're going to neutralize your home so that anybody walking through your door could visualize themselves all cozy and settled in right away!

In this guide, you will find I've covered a lot of ground, but don't get overwhelmed. Take it step by step and you'll be fine. Next to each category you will see an empty box that you can check off once you've tackled that specific topic. Hopefully, you'll discover that you have already taken care of some of these things and your tasks at hand will seem a little less daunting.

Before you embark on your journey of sprucing up your house, there is one important thing you need to ask yourself: Is your house priced to sell? Not just the price that *you* feel it is worth, but a number that supports what the market is doing in your area. I am not a realtor or an appraiser, so you should consult with one of these professionals to obtain the fair market value of your home; that way you can insure that it has the appropriate price tag on it.

Okay, you are ready to go, so let's roll up our sleeves and get down to business! Grab a pencil and check off the boxes as you go through the guide, and don't get overwhelmed. You can do it! Good luck!!

GETTING STARTED

☐ With your guide and a pencil in hand, let's get started on this journey to getting your house sold! The first thing on your "to do" list is to **find someone who can give you an objective opinion** on every category in this guide. I will refer to this objective opinion person as your **OP** throughout the book. This can be a friend, a neighbor or a family member and, because you are placing a lot of trust in this person, please make sure they have good taste. That sounds harsh, huh? Well, you are counting on their comments, opinions and suggestions, so them having good taste is kind of a prerequisite for the job.

I cannot express how invaluable this person will be to you, so be prepared for a little constructive criticism. Do not take any ideas or opinions given to you by this person personally! Your OP is going to help you see things you normally would not. Many times we get so used to things around us, we cannot see that they are in need of repair or changing. I have even used an OP per the request of my husband. I really didn't think I needed anybody's opinion on the placement of my furniture or the wall color in my living room because, come on, I've got good taste. Well, I still think I've got good taste, but somebody else's perspective was just what I needed. Put your pride aside and find yourself an OP.

☐ The second thing to do is **find a store that has a good home decorating magazine selection.** In addition to your OP, these magazines will be a huge asset to you in selling your house. There are pages and pages of ideas to point you in the right direction - from paint color to decorating your mantle. I always refer to my magazines if I am stuck when trying to rearrange a room, or just do something different in there. There is such an unbelievable selection of home décor magazines out there that it will boggle your mind as to which ones to choose. Just about any one of these will work for you with the exception being a magazine that sports ultra modern design. When choosing a good magazine you'll want to stay with the more traditional styles. If this was your house you were staying in the rest of your life, then I'd say, "Go big!" and do what you want. However, that's not the case, so let's stay traditional.

Feel free to e-mail me at <u>sell-your-house@hotmail.com</u>, and I will forward you a list of the magazines that I use for reference on a daily basis. Any of these magazines would work great to help you achieve your goal in selling your house.

☐ **Make note of your home's appealing qualities** - If there is anything that is of significance to you about your home and you feel like it could sway the homebuyer in your direction, then by all means make sure your realtor is aware of it. My husband and I are going to be selling our current house in the spring and we already have a "perks" list that we'll leave sitting out for people to look at. What do you put on a "perks" list, you ask? Well, with our home, one of its greatest attributes is that it faces west. Who cares, you say? Well, when you want to relax with a glass of wine after a long day of work, or you want to have a BBQ in the late afternoon in the summer, we don't have the hot afternoon sun glaring down on us, because it has been blocked by our house! *Bonus*! We may not have appreciated this if we had not previously had a house that received hot afternoon sun on the back deck, and we couldn't go sit out there until the sun went down!

We also live on the side of the street without a sidewalk, and this is a wonderful thing in the winter when it snows. No sidewalk means NO SHOVELING! In states where it snows a lot, there is usually a city ordinance that requires you to shovel your walk or else you get fined.

Some other good qualities for your house may be:
- The proximity to the schools
- The great school system
- The proximity to parks
- The local recreation center for the family
- An instant heat system for the water
- Perennial flowerbeds

If there are things about your home that you feel are important, don't underestimate their appeal to others. Write them down!

☐ **Take pictures** - Take pictures of your house when it is at its peak. Your house may have the most beautiful trees in the fall, the greenest grass in the summer, a gorgeous bed of roses when in bloom, and you may even have a picturesque landscape in the winter. Whatever the season, when your home looks its best, inside or out, you'll want to create a scrapbook to show potential homebuyers what they have to look forward to.

THE OUTSIDE

We are going to start outside at the far end of your driveway, on the sidewalk in front or on the street facing your home. Be safe, smart, and please don't stand in the middle of the street! Here we go.

ROOFING

☐ **Roof repair** - Do you have leaks in your roof? Do you have shingles that are loose or have come off completely? There is a simple solution to these problems - fix them. The damaged shingles on your roof are not appealing to the eye and even if the shingles pose no threat when it is raining, they need to be repaired immediately. Hire this one out or do it yourself – your choice, but it has to be done.

☐ **Mildew or mold on your roof** - I always thought those awful streaks running down the front or back of the roof was tar seeping through, but no, it was mold! If you have this problem with your roof, you need to address it. You can attempt this venture on your own, but working on top of your house can be very dangerous, so I recommend calling a roofing company and getting their opinion. A professional can assess the situation and who knows, it may call for more than what you are willing (or capable) of doing. You may even have extensive roof damage and not know it. However, if you do decide to tackle this project on your own, please proceed with caution. Use a pressure washer with a mild bleach solution. Start out with the pressure washer on the lowest setting and spray down the roof, towards the gutter. For really heavy mold, you are better off consulting a professional.

☐ **Gutters** - If you have gutters on your home, then you'll need to assess their condition. Check real good to make sure that your gutters and down spouts are not dented or bent. Damaged goods are no good, so if they are in need of repair or replacing, make sure you take the proper steps. Your larger home improvement stores will have everything you need to get the job done right. You may only have a few nicks, wear or fading of color on your gutters and if this is the case, we are going to tackle that problem later on when we talk about painting the house.

☐ **Are your gutters clean?** - If you have a lot of trees or your neighbor does, then chances are you have leaves, sticks and maybe a little mulch in your gutters. Check it out and have them cleaned out. I can't say it enough—be careful!

☐ **From fascia and trim molding to shutters** - Paint always seems like the logical fix, but make sure they are not in need of some repair or need to be replaced. The outside elements can wreck havoc on wood shutters, trim around windows, fascia and soffets.

☐ **Leaf guards** - If you have gutters and if you have trees, then these little babies are a must! All you have to do is pop some inexpensive leaf guards in your gutters and wow, what a difference, no more compost in the gutters! Leaf guards are available at your local home improvement stores and are very reasonable. Hint: I would put this one on my perks list.

☐ **Debris** - If you have sticks or loose leaves on or in the valleys of your roof, then you'll have to get that crap off there. It's unsightly for one, and it gives an appearance of neglect. Be extremely careful up there or hire it out if you're not comfortable with this one. Personally, I'm afraid of heights, so I would have someone else do this for me!

DRIVEWAYS

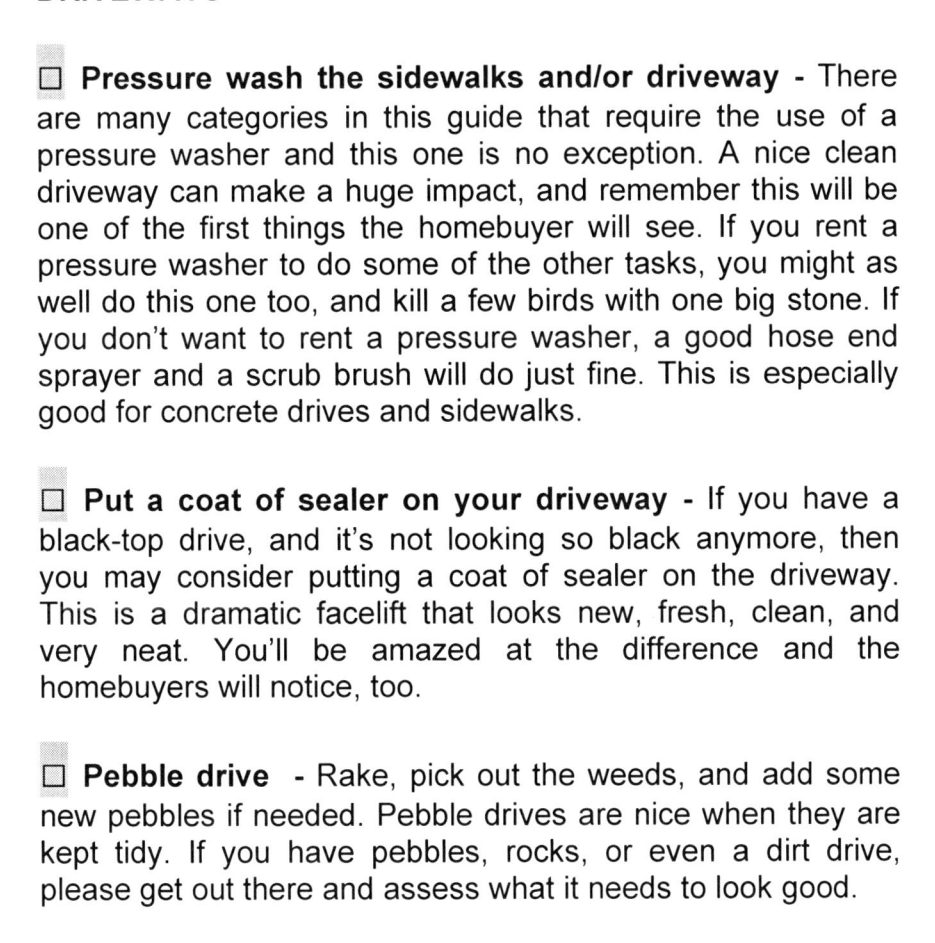

☐ **Pressure wash the sidewalks and/or driveway** - There are many categories in this guide that require the use of a pressure washer and this one is no exception. A nice clean driveway can make a huge impact, and remember this will be one of the first things the homebuyer will see. If you rent a pressure washer to do some of the other tasks, you might as well do this one too, and kill a few birds with one big stone. If you don't want to rent a pressure washer, a good hose end sprayer and a scrub brush will do just fine. This is especially good for concrete drives and sidewalks.

☐ **Put a coat of sealer on your driveway** - If you have a black-top drive, and it's not looking so black anymore, then you may consider putting a coat of sealer on the driveway. This is a dramatic facelift that looks new, fresh, clean, and very neat. You'll be amazed at the difference and the homebuyers will notice, too.

☐ **Pebble drive** - Rake, pick out the weeds, and add some new pebbles if needed. Pebble drives are nice when they are kept tidy. If you have pebbles, rocks, or even a dirt drive, please get out there and assess what it needs to look good.

LAWNS

☐ **Mow your grass** - I can't emphasize this enough. Mow, mow, and mow some more! So many homes are up for sale and the grass is as high as the mailbox, and then when they finally decide to mow, they end up scalping the poor lawn! Don't do this. You want to be consistent about keeping it cut, this will make for a more luscious lawn. I have Kentucky Fescue grass and in the summer I mow my grass at least twice a week, and I have a thick gorgeous lawn! Ask a local nursery or landscape company about the proper mowing heights for the type of grass you have. We all live in different regions of the country and have different grass, which can require very different care.

☐ **Fertilize your lawn** - The type of grass you have and the time of year it is will regulate whether or not to fertilize. Every lawn needs it, and it may be the perfect time for you to do it. Check with your local nursery or a landscape company about fertilizing the type of grass you have. A well-fed lawn is a happy lawn!

☐ **Reseed your lawn** - This is another one that will require knowing the type of grass you have. You may not even need to do this, so get a professional opinion to be on the safe side. If you find that you need to reseed, it's not a daunting task to do on your own. You can get some great advice from your local nursery.

☐ **Water your lawn and flower beds** - This is a must, folks! I know there have been quite a bit of water restrictions all over the country because of a lack of rain during the summer months. Where I live, starting Memorial Day to Labor Day, there is an odd-even watering cycle, so if your house number is an odd number, then you water on odd days. Whenever you're allowed to water, then you must do it! A brown lawn and drooping plants would turn any homebuyer in another direction.

☐ **Weeding** - Dandelions are not flowers! I've seen some lawns that if they were a flower, those folks could pick a fresh bouquet every day for their entire neighborhood! Even if you have a green thumb, everybody has a few weeds pop up now and then. If you have weeds, get rid of them. Please don't go and just spray anything on them; ask your local nursery what they suggest, or if you feel like you need some good exercise, then pull them up by hand. They make some pretty nifty weed-pulling gadgets these days and they're very user-friendly.

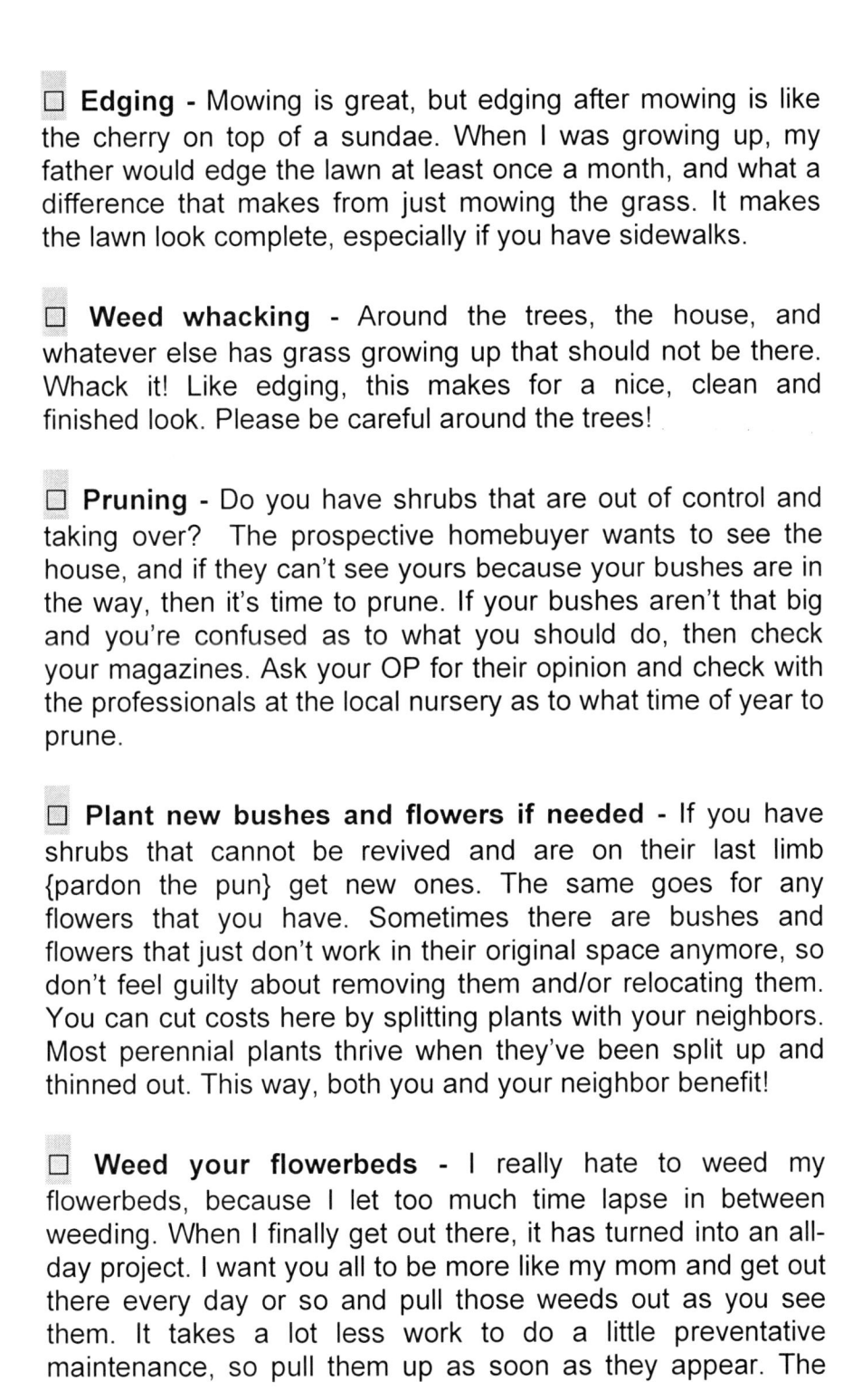

☐ **Edging** - Mowing is great, but edging after mowing is like the cherry on top of a sundae. When I was growing up, my father would edge the lawn at least once a month, and what a difference that makes from just mowing the grass. It makes the lawn look complete, especially if you have sidewalks.

☐ **Weed whacking** - Around the trees, the house, and whatever else has grass growing up that should not be there. Whack it! Like edging, this makes for a nice, clean and finished look. Please be careful around the trees!

☐ **Pruning** - Do you have shrubs that are out of control and taking over? The prospective homebuyer wants to see the house, and if they can't see yours because your bushes are in the way, then it's time to prune. If your bushes aren't that big and you're confused as to what you should do, then check your magazines. Ask your OP for their opinion and check with the professionals at the local nursery as to what time of year to prune.

☐ **Plant new bushes and flowers if needed** - If you have shrubs that cannot be revived and are on their last limb {pardon the pun} get new ones. The same goes for any flowers that you have. Sometimes there are bushes and flowers that just don't work in their original space anymore, so don't feel guilty about removing them and/or relocating them. You can cut costs here by splitting plants with your neighbors. Most perennial plants thrive when they've been split up and thinned out. This way, both you and your neighbor benefit!

☐ **Weed your flowerbeds** - I really hate to weed my flowerbeds, because I let too much time lapse in between weeding. When I finally get out there, it has turned into an all-day project. I want you all to be more like my mom and get out there every day or so and pull those weeds out as you see them. It takes a lot less work to do a little preventative maintenance, so pull them up as soon as they appear. The bonus is looking at your beautiful flowers every day. The homebuyers will like it, too!

☐ **Gardens** - Do you have a vegetable or flower garden? Are these garden spaces well defined? Does your garden spill out onto your lawn to the point that when you cut the grass you are mowing over squash or daisies along with the grass? These areas of your yard should be well-defined spaces with some type of mulch or edging. Consult with your OP and look in your magazines so that you can visualize how to define the areas in your garden.

PORCHES

Whether you have a big 'ole southern front porch or a small simple concrete slab, you are going to want to dress it up and make it as inviting as you can. Remember, this is one of the first places the homebuyer sees and one of the last, so we want to make a lasting impression, and a good one at that.

☐ **Flowers on your front porch** - You don't need a field of flowers on the front porch; just a couple of containers on either side of your front door will do the trick. There are many varieties to choose from, but some of my favorites are geraniums, petunias, and impatients. Pack your containers full to give a dramatic effect. If flowers aren't an option because it's wintertime, no problem! Simply put together a seasonal bouquet of evergreen cuttings, pinecones and berries. Every fall and winter all the nurseries have these supplies ready and available, and if you are not up to the task, then purchase a pre-made arrangement. Please be careful not to overdo it with the plants. It's easy to get out of control with plants and flowers and before you know it, you have a jungle on your front porch. You want the flowers to enhance the beauty of you entrance, not overwhelm it. By the way, absolutely no fake flowers.

☐ **Flowerpots -** What your plants go in is almost as important as the plants themselves. My advice is to stay neutral here and maintain a theme of terra cotta, and the pots can be clay or plastic. They make some very believable faux clay pots for a fraction of the price of clay. Another alternative that is very affordable is spray paint! Some brands of spray paint actually make a terra cotta color, and that way you can insure that all your pots match!

☐ **Decks -** If you have a deck, then let's take a look at its condition. Has it been painted, stained or clear-coated with weather sealer? If it has been painted, then how does it look? If it's in great shape, then that is awesome news for you. However, if there is paint flaking off anywhere, then you'll want to pressure wash that off and put a coat of paint on, if not two. If your stained deck is looking a little faded, then you'll want to follow the same steps as above and pressure wash first before applying new stain or weather sealer.
Of course if there are any repairs that need to be made to your deck, then do it!

☐ **Stain front walk and/or front and back patio -** If you have a concrete walk up to your front door and/or a concrete patio in the front or the back of your house, then you may want to consider staining them. It truly makes for a rich, welcoming feeling and gives added dimension to an otherwise boring slab of concrete. Check with your paint professional for any needed advice on what color and type of stain would work best for you. Remember to keep it neutral!

☐ **Stage your porch -** Your front porch and/or back patio or deck needs to feel like it's truly an extension of your inside living area. Create this feeling by having comfortable seating, a small table to hold a drink, and maybe even an outside area rug to tie everything together. Add a few candles, some potted plants and there you have it, a wonderful outside room!

Keep in mind that the same rules for the inside of your home apply to the outside, so you'll want to have furniture that fits the scale of the living area, and the pieces should coordinate with each other. I'm not a stickler for 'matching' pieces of furniture, but they should go well with each other. If you're unsure how they look together, then pull them together with matching throw pillows, take a step back, and then see how they look. Still stumped? Pull out those magazines; they're full of outside living area ideas.

☐ **Welcome mats** - A simple mat made of natural fibers works great, and let's keep it uncluttered of anything other than the word "WELCOME". Mats get worn out fairly quickly due to the outside elements, so I would suggest investing in a new one for each entrance to your home. They are quite affordable and make the welcome to your home a warm one.

OUTSIDE STRUCTURES

☐ **Fences** - If you have a fence, assess whether it needs to be repaired, pressure washed or painted.

☐ **Sheds** - If you have a shed, then you need to take a good hard look at it and determine what kind of shape it's in. Is your shed in good shape, does it need some repair or is it beyond repair? Do you need to consider taking it down and replacing it, or taking it down and not replace it? A dilapidated shed is an eyesore, not to mention extra work in the homebuyer's mind.

On a different note, could it just use a new coat of paint? Does the color on your shed match the color of your house? Now, the shed color does not necessarily have to match the color of the house, but it does give some continuity.

You've got a few things to consider here, so my suggestion would be to check your magazines for ideas. They are chock full of outdoor design ideas that involve outdoor structures, such as sheds. Who knows, maybe you just need to plant some flowers and shrubs around it!

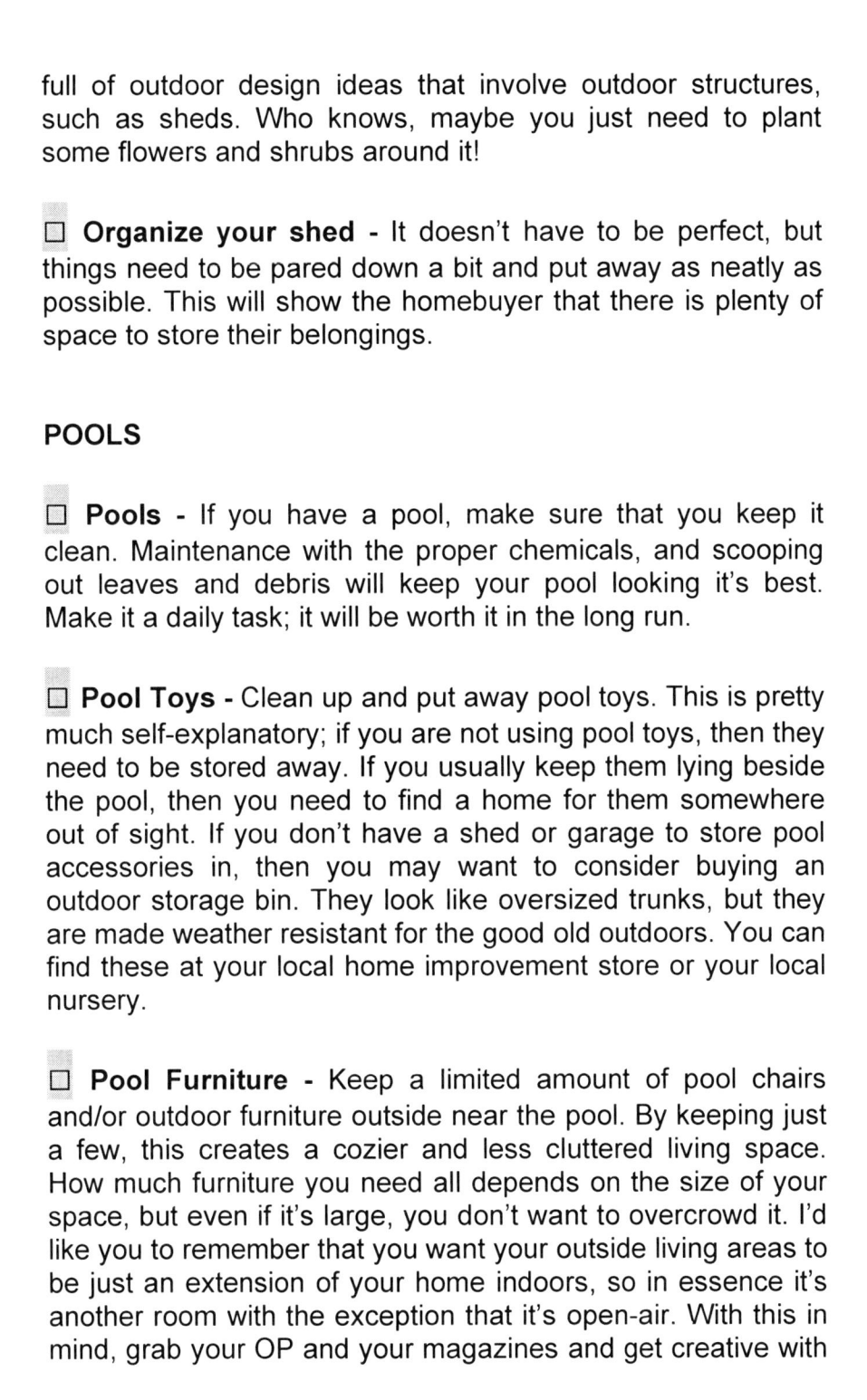

☐ **Organize your shed** - It doesn't have to be perfect, but things need to be pared down a bit and put away as neatly as possible. This will show the homebuyer that there is plenty of space to store their belongings.

POOLS

☐ **Pools** - If you have a pool, make sure that you keep it clean. Maintenance with the proper chemicals, and scooping out leaves and debris will keep your pool looking it's best. Make it a daily task; it will be worth it in the long run.

☐ **Pool Toys** - Clean up and put away pool toys. This is pretty much self-explanatory; if you are not using pool toys, then they need to be stored away. If you usually keep them lying beside the pool, then you need to find a home for them somewhere out of sight. If you don't have a shed or garage to store pool accessories in, then you may want to consider buying an outdoor storage bin. They look like oversized trunks, but they are made weather resistant for the good old outdoors. You can find these at your local home improvement store or your local nursery.

☐ **Pool Furniture** - Keep a limited amount of pool chairs and/or outdoor furniture outside near the pool. By keeping just a few, this creates a cozier and less cluttered living space. How much furniture you need all depends on the size of your space, but even if it's large, you don't want to overcrowd it. I'd like you to remember that you want your outside living areas to be just an extension of your home indoors, so in essence it's another room with the exception that it's open-air. With this in mind, grab your OP and your magazines and get creative with

13

the placement of your outdoor furniture. Hint: Try to arrange furniture in a manner that encourages conversation.

GARAGES

☐ **Clean and Organize** - Most garages are the catchall for everything! At least mine is! It seems to be that if you can't find a home for something, into the garage it goes. This makes it difficult to clean with all that extra stuff in the way. A great solution for storing your belongings in a neat and tidy way is the use of plastic tubs with lids. They come in a variety of colors and sizes, and are great at keeping your things super organized. My husband and I use different colored bins to distinguish between our things. For example, we use red bins for all of our Christmas stuff and we use gray bins for our camping gear. Like I said before, you really can get them in just about every color and size imaginable. You know, since you're going to the trouble to get organized, really try to make a concerted effort to keep things in place. I know this can be hard for some folks (like me), especially when you're in a hurry, but there are a couple of benefits to this. For one, it is very attractive to the homebuyer to see the garage neat and organized and all the space that is available to them. However, the best incentive for staying organized is that it will make it a cinch to move when you sell your house!

☐ **Paint the garage floor** - Think about it. If your vehicle left the floor soiled, then painting may be something to consider. First, try to scrub the soiled area with some degreaser to see if you can get it clean. Helpful hint: Cat liter works great to absorb grease; just spread it over the greasy area and work it into the spot with your shoe.
Even if the garage floor is not heavily soiled, painting can still give it an awesome facelift. There are so many options when it comes to garage floor paint these days. You can get paint with speckles, textured non-skid surface paint and so much more, so check with your local home improvement store for your

choices. Some stores hire out and will even do the work for you if you're not up to the task. Additional fees may apply, so check with the pros for prices. If you do decide to do this yourself, use only paint that is made specifically for garage floors and follow all manufacturers instructions. Do not use latex paint on your garage floor, as you will have a huge mess if you do.

☐ **Garage walls** - Could you possibly finish and/or paint the interior walls of your garage? Check out the situation and call in your OP for some helpful advice. Since this is in your garage, it's not mandatory to do this. However, this is something I'd like you to just consider.

☐ **Heating your garage** - Again, this is not something that you have to do, but if you live where I live, this is a definite perk! Let's say I was looking to buy a house up in my neck of the woods and I narrowed my search down to two choices and for argument's sake, they were identical houses. The only difference between the two houses was that one had a heated garage. Well not just me, but anyone up north would choose the house with the heated garage! Since living up in Minnesota where in the winter your garage doubles as a freezer, I've come to appreciate the heated garage. I've also learned that the garage is party central up here (maybe it's just the heated ones)!

At least for folks living in the upper Mid-west, this should be considered on your to-do list when getting your house "for sale" worthy. Inquire about your options at your local home improvement store.

WINDOWS

☐ **Clean your windows** - What a difference this makes! Clean the windows, inside and out. You may not realize how dirty they really are until you've cleaned them, so please, get that window cleaner out and clean those windows!

☐ **Clean or replace the window screens** - Replace your screens if you have tears, rips, big holes, etc. Consider cleaning your screens if needed. If you have windows that are low to the ground, they probably need to be cleaned more often due to dirt and/or mud that splatters onto them.

☐ **Re-glaze and/or replace panes and sashes** - With older homes come older windows, and they may require a little tender love and care. Even if your house is not on the historic route through town, your windows may still need some updating. My advice for this subject would be to call in a professional to see what kind of maintenance your windows require. Efficient windows could be a definite plus in a homebuyer's eye, yet you don't want to break the bank with unnecessary upgrades. The professionals at your local home improvement stores and exclusive window stores give great advice no matter what your budget is.

PAINTING

☐ **Pressure wash your house** - It's amazing what pressure washing the house can do! This is great for vinyl siding and brick. Contact a professional for stucco and painted houses. The process for cleaning those surfaces may be quite different. If you can pressure wash your house, it can look as though you've recently painted it. Using a pressure washer can be very simple, but you want to exercise extreme caution and start on the lowest setting. You don't want to blast the siding off your house.

☐ **Paint** - I have seen countless houses for sale that really need a different color on them. Ask yourself this question: Does your house need a fresh coat of paint, or maybe an updated new color? If your 'self' is not giving you an honest answer, then ask your OP! It's fine if you have an unusual or uncommon color on your house and you never plan on moving, although that's too bad for your neighbors.

So, what color to paint? This is another good task for your OP, your magazines and the paint professionals at your local home improvement store or paint store. You do want to neutralize the color pallet a little with more earth tone shades, such as different variations of white, just about anything in the brown family, and some grays. Do a little research by looking through some magazines to find similar houses to yours. You can also stroll through your own, or neighboring, neighborhoods to get some good ideas. With some help from you, paint professionals can give you some color suggestions that will suit your house perfectly.

☐ **Paint the trim** - The above applies to this category as well; they kind of go hand in hand, so try to keep it neutral. If you don't need to paint your house, maybe your trim just needs a little sprucing up. If your trim does need a fresh coat and you don't want to change the color, paint professionals can match your existing trim color near perfect.

☐ **Paint light fixtures** - I am a huge fan of spray paint and its many uses, and this category is no exception. If you really don't care for those outside light fixtures, instead of buying new ones, just change the color of them. You can really give those tired, outdated light fixtures new life and make them look brand new! They make spray paint in so many different finishes now that the sky's the limit. Why spend money on new lights when a can of spray paint can bring them up to date! All you need is a well-ventilated area, some newspaper for over spray and voila! It looks as though you went out and bought new light fixtures and all you spent was a whopping $3.50!

MISCELLANEOUS OUTSIDE

☐ **Outside lights** - This is a no-brainer; replace light bulbs that are burned out and repair broken lights if needed.

☐ **Doorbell** - Does the doorbell work? If it doesn't, fix it. Is the button that you push in good shape? Check it out, and if it needs to be replaced you can find them at your local home improvement store at a bargain price.

☐ **Clean your grill** - Everything should be clean and neat! If you have a cover for your grill, use it, because it just looks better. If you don't have a cover for your grill, then I suggest investing in one to keep your grill in good shape. I have another suggestion in the event that your grill is looking kind of grungy. You guessed it: spray paint it!! They make applicable paint to handle the heat, but ask the sales associate at your local home improvement store to assure you are getting the correct paint. This inexpensive project can get that old grill looking brand new!

☐ **Pick up pet droppings** - Everyone knows what this means: pick up your dog's poop! Do it everyday, folks, especially if you have a big dog or multiple dogs.

☐ **No yard toys!** - Put kids' toys in the shed or garage, at least when they are done playing with them.

☐ **No political signs in the yard** - You could really turn off a potential homebuyer with your political opinion, so your best bet is to keep it to yourself.

☐ **Personal signs** - What I mean by this are the family name signs and signs that have sayings on them. You want to create an environment that lets the homebuyers picture themselves in this house, and having your last name posted won't allow them to do that. Many of these signs appear kind of cutesy and a bit cluttery. Don't take it personally. We have one that my son made for us with an old piece of wood and a wood burner, and it's displayed proudly near our front door. However, when it comes time to sell our house, it will be lovingly packed away.

☐ **Hang an American flag** - The American dream is to own a house, so it just makes sense to have a flag hanging outside. When I see an American flag hanging outside someone's house, it makes me feel good and it makes that home look complete. Put one up and see how it makes you feel. I bet the homebuyers will feel the same way.

☐ **Yard art** - I've gone back and forth about this category so many times that it makes my head spin! When I first wrote this I said no yard art at all, but there are things out there that can enhance your landscape. Yard art comes in many different forms from gazing balls to stone statues to birdhouses. You will need to pack some of these things up so be selective about what you keep out, because too much can look real tacky. You'll also want to make sure that what you do keep out is in good taste and is not distracting in any way.

My personal opinion is that the front yard is not a place for these things. I would recommend that you put away any yard art that you have out front and what you do decide to keep out, reserve it for the backyard only.

☐ **The mailbox** - What kind of condition is your mailbox in? Does it need to be replaced, or would a little spray paint help it out? Make sure that the numbers on your box are in good condition as well. If you need new numbers you can go to your local home improvement store. They have a great selection of styles and colors at bargain prices.

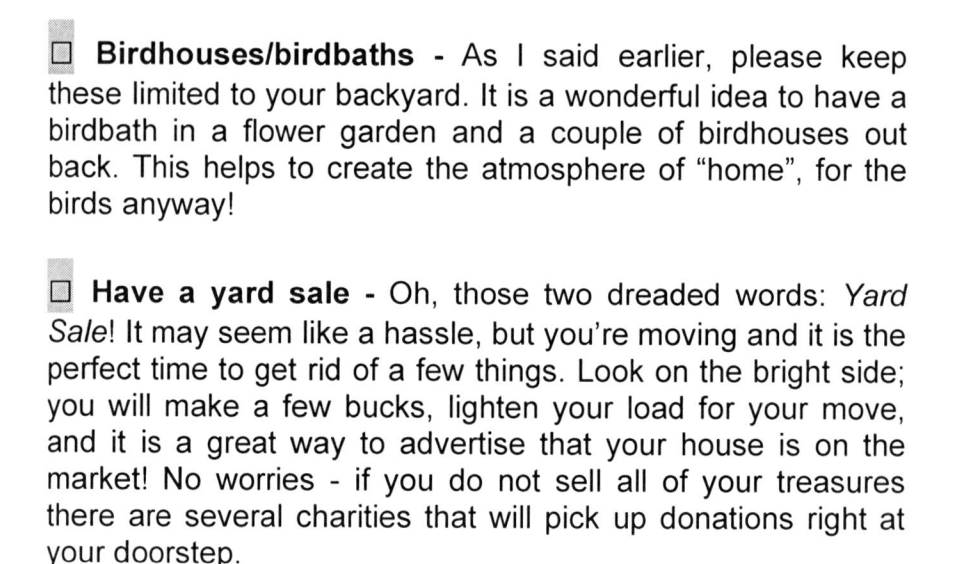

☐ **Birdhouses/birdbaths** - As I said earlier, please keep these limited to your backyard. It is a wonderful idea to have a birdbath in a flower garden and a couple of birdhouses out back. This helps to create the atmosphere of "home", for the birds anyway!

☐ **Have a yard sale** - Oh, those two dreaded words: *Yard Sale*! It may seem like a hassle, but you're moving and it is the perfect time to get rid of a few things. Look on the bright side; you will make a few bucks, lighten your load for your move, and it is a great way to advertise that your house is on the market! No worries - if you do not sell all of your treasures there are several charities that will pick up donations right at your doorstep.

THE INSIDE

BEFORE YOU DO ANYTHING!

Stop here and take a step back for a moment. I want to explain how we're going to tackle the inside so you'll better understand the method of my madness. There is a certain process we'll go through inside and to achieve the maximum result, you'll really want to stay true to these steps, so try real hard not to jump ahead. Now if you've already gone through these steps, then by all means, plow forward.
Here we go!

DE-CLUTTERFY!

Okay, we are going to tackle the most difficult thing in this book: your stuff! We'll walk through the steps you'll take to get the task done.

Have fun going down memory lane, but keep in mind that you want to go through your belongings relatively quickly. If you dwell too long, you have too much time to think and then you'll never get rid of anything! Trust me, I know this first hand. I can't even attend my own yard sales or I'll buy my own stuff!

☐ **Clutter** - Before we start with any room, you're going to have to empty it. Yep, you heard me right. You're going to have to devote a little time to this task, because it's not as simple as moving all your stuff to another room. No, you're going to go through all your stuff first. Everybody has some kind of clutter. If you don't, then you are the exception. Clutter takes on all forms, from loose paperwork to knick-knack collections, or a pile of shoes by the front door, to too much furniture. Basically, too much of anything is considered clutter. Wherever the clutter may lie in your home, it's time to get rid of it. Now, I'm not saying that you have to get rid of all your belongings forever, but it needs to at least be stored away while you're selling your house. To make life a little easier and the task at hand a little less daunting, I want you to go through your things and divide them into three different piles: one to put in your yard sale and whatever is left after the sale you can donate to charity; one to toss in the garbage; and one to keep. Once you've done this, scan over your piles once more and make sure that you're only keeping things you love, use and are functional. Put those last items I mentioned aside for the time being. We'll need them at the end of the book when we address decorating your space.

☐ **Collections** - In a perfect world it would not matter what is sitting out; people would look right past it and buy your house anyway. In our less than perfect world of real estate investing, people may look at some of your things and cringe. Remember what I told you from the beginning, that most people cannot see beyond what is in front of them at that moment; hence they will not be able to see past your collection of shot glasses. This is not a personal stab at anyone with collections no matter what they are, this is simply allowing the prospective homebuyer to focus on the house as it fits their needs, not your own. The homebuyer needs to see the potential of the living space for their belongings and sometimes it's hard to look past certain things. Okay, let's get down to it - what goes and what stays? If you have a shrine devoted to the Denver Broncos in the corner of your living room (this is how my husband would have it), then it goes. If you have every Hummel made, it's time to sort through and display a few chosen pieces, preferably in a curio cabinet. This goes for any kind of figurine that you might collect. I collect old decanters for liquor and wine. They are usually crystal and very pretty, but I don't keep them all out at the same time, and

I do keep them grouped together. Use this as an opportunity to pack up you collections, since you are moving anyway. This is also a great opportunity to ask yourself if you really want to keep those collections. Like I said before, what you don't want to keep you can sell, donate or toss. Less is more, and the less stuff you have crowding your room the bigger your room appears, and the less stuff you keep, the less stuff you have to move!

☐ **Furniture, artwork, etc.** – Go through these items and decide what you truly don't like or will not use anymore. Take these things and put them in your yard sale, donate them to charity, or simply toss what is broken and not repairable. Hang on to the remaining items you're keeping and put them aside while we work on the next section. After we've addressed all the steps in the next few categories, then we'll refer to the decorating section near the end of the book, and at this point we will decide what items to keep out for display and what to pack up.

FOYERS/ENTRYWAY

☐ **The foyer** - When you walk into your home, what does your entry look like? Are you walking right onto the carpet or do you have different flooring to define the space. The problem I've noticed with a lot of houses is that there is no definitive area between the front door entry and the living room. A lot of times this is because the carpeting goes all the way to the front door, and that can make for some badly soiled carpet. Even if you have a small house with a small living room, you can define your entry with a small area of different flooring. Simply lay ceramic tile in front of the door just enough to define the entry to the house. This will help keep dirty feet off the carpet and it's fairly inexpensive. Consider other areas i.e. in the front of a sliding glass door or the back entry of the house. You don't have to use ceramic tile, there are many flooring options available to you such as laminate wood flooring and vinyl tile.

Many local home improvement stores offer free classes on how to lay ceramic tile and wood floors. Recruit a friend to help and the project won't seem so scary.

☐ **Closets** - This is the first place the homebuyer will look for coat and shoe storage, so let's start out with a good impression. You're just going to start here, because all the closets in your home deserve the same attention. Go through every closet in your house no matter how scared you are of opening that door! Remember that people will be opening up those doors to see how much space they contain. This is a good time to gather more things for your upcoming yard sale and thin out your closet squatters; you know those things that go in your closet and never come out! Once you have gone through everything and you are ready to put your things back, give careful thought as to how it is placed. Like the rest of the rooms in the house, we want your closets to appear as spacious as can be.

FLOORS

Since we're already talking about flooring in the entryway, I figured we'd just stay on the subject for a while. First we need to consider what kind of floors you currently have and then assess whether or not they are working for your space.

☐ **Carpet** - If you have carpet anywhere in your home, then we need to take a good look at it to see what kind of condition it's in. The condition and color of your carpet will determine if it stays or if it goes.

First question: What color is your carpet? We want to stay as neutral as we can here and if you have anything outside of earth tone shades, then you may want to consider replacing it if it's within your budget. You may also want to consider changing your carpet out if it is different everywhere in the house. Having the same color carpet throughout the house creates continuity, which invites a nice flow throughout. I know that can make you cringe, but if you have blue, green, yellow, well you get the picture, that is simply going to be a negative in the homebuyer's mind, and even more so if it's broken up throughout the house. Great! Now if you are indeed facing the fact that you need new carpet don't fret, for there are so many options available to you. Talk to the carpet professionals at your local home improvement stores about your options. Carpet is very affordable if you're looking in the right direction. Check out remnants or carpet tiles and find out what's on sale. They are always running specials on certain carpets and installation. Don't settle! Shop around and find the best deal for you!

Second question: What's the condition of your carpet? Are there big holes or tears in your carpeting? Do you have stains that you can't get out? When selling your house, you simply cannot have crappy carpet. Period. I have a couple of great solutions to solve some of your less problematic issues, such as a tiny permanent spot or hole, and this is a fairly easy repair. Here's how: Find a spot in your carpet where you can take a little bit of carpeting without it being noticed. Very carefully, cut out a few strands, place a dab of hot glue on the end, and place in the hole. Hole repaired!

Third question: What's underneath your carpet? Take a peep and check it out. If you have salvageable hardwood floors lying beneath, then you should strongly consider taking the carpet up and letting the wood take center stage. That is a big plus to homebuyers and who knows, you may discover all they need is to be buffed out.

Have your carpet cleaned by a professional. What a difference this can make! There are carpet cleaners that you can rent if you're up to the task and they are quite affordable, or you may have a friend or family member that owns their own cleaner and would loan it to you. Whatever the case, the shampoo cleaners and accessories are available to you at your local home improvement store. However, this is one project where I would call in the professionals. For one, they are always running specials and offering coupons in the mail or the paper, and two, they do all the clean up!

☐ **Hard surface flooring** - If you have ceramic tile in your home and some of the tile is cracked, outdated, or just plain ugly, you need to see about replacing them. If you have hardwood floors, check their condition. If you come across a lot of scratches or gouges, you may want to see about having them refinished or just buffed out. This can possibly be a do-it-yourselfer job if you're up for it. Check with your local home improvement store to see if they offer rental services and if they do, then you're in luck! For a fraction of the price and a little elbow grease, you can have beautiful hardwood floors.

For vinyl tile or linoleum floors you will be looking for the same thing, along with discoloration, and ground-in dirt that you just cannot get clean. If this is the case with your vinyl flooring you will need to replace it. Not to worry. They have a huge selection of vinyl flooring at your larger home improvement stores, and they are pretty user-friendly to install and very affordable! A majority of the time, you can even lay new flooring right on top of the old. I have done that before and if I can do it, anyone can do it!

You may want to consider hardwood laminate flooring as a flooring option, too. They are very beautiful, easy to install, super durable and you can't beat the price.

☐ **Area rugs** - Area rugs are a great way to pull a room together and add warmth, and you can use them on any hard-surfaced floor and even on carpeting. The colors, patterns and sizes that are available are limitless and very affordable. Check your Sunday paper for sales! You can also e-mail me at sell-your-house@hotmail.com and I'll send you a list of my favorite stores to shop for rugs.

Keep in mind that when you use area rugs you need to have it anchored down with furniture or else it gets lost and the room loses the cozy factor. A good rule to follow is to have at least one foot from a couple of pieces of furniture surrounding the rug, on the rug.

WALLS AND WALL COLOR

☐ **Wall repair** - Before we talk about color, let's first look at the condition of your walls. Is there damage from things being bumped into the wall, small nail holes or even large nail holes? These things need to be taken care of and it's easy enough that anyone can do it. For almost any size hole all you need is some lightweight Spackle, a putty knife and some fine grit sandpaper. Larger holes may require a piece of sheetrock to fill the hole and sheetrock mud. They sell small kits especially for this type of project. All these supplies can be found at your local home improvement store and while you're there just ask the pros for any advice if you need it. Keep in mind that this step must be done before applying paint to your walls.

☐ **To paint or not to paint** - If you have little children, and it's been a while since you've painted, then I would be willing to guess the walls need a refresher. Even if you don't have little ones, take a good look at your walls to determine if you need a fresh coat of paint. I'd be willing to bet they do and they probably need an update on the color as well. Good! Now that you've decided that you need to paint, you need to decide on a color that will sell your house well. What's a 'sellable' color, you say? There are a lot of options when it comes to color, so let's explore this more in the next category.

☐ **What color?** - We want to stay close to the rules that we applied to the outside of your home when it comes to color. What we don't want are funky colors such as royal blue, canary yellow, lime green, purple in any shade, pinks and oranges. It doesn't matter how much you love these colors, because more than likely the homebuyer will not. The goal here is to neutralize the color pallet so that potential homebuyers that walk through your door can picture themselves in your home without having to change a thing, and having a neutral backdrop is the first step. Remember this: The less work a homebuyer has to do, the less time it takes for them to think about buying your house. On that note, what we do want are shades of beige, tan and gray-greens, such as sage, browns and off-whites. These colors achieve warmth and drama with easy on the eyes earth tones, and they will work in any room in your house. Now, if you're drawn to whites, please make sure that it is not stark white. Try to stay with shades that resemble beach sand, that will give you your white without that sterile hospital feel.

When choosing a color, you'll also want to keep in mind the furniture that will be going in the respective room. If you keep to the neutral tones for wall color, then just about any piece of furniture should work nicely. We'll talk more about furniture and accessories later.

Okay, let's get busy! Search through your home decorating magazines, grab your OP, and head for your local home improvement store for some paint swatches.

☐ **Ceiling color** - So, you've got your head turned upward and you're saying to yourself: "*I don't know when they were painted last, but I think my ceilings look just fine.*" Try this little test - go to your local home improvement store and buy some white ceiling paint. Pick a room that is fairly small, maybe a bathroom, because once you start this little test, you really must finish. Put the first roller of paint on the ceiling. Then decide whether or not your ceilings need to be painted. More than likely the shades will be very different between your original ceiling color and the white you just rolled on. You'll really notice a difference if you've had smokers living in your house! Hint: Stick to white paint on your ceilings when selling your house. It's a safe hue and will go with anything.

☐ **Trim molding** - Living in Minnesota, I've noticed that most new homes have wood-stained trim, as opposed to when I lived in Georgia. Many of the houses there have white trim molding. Whatever you have in your home, you need to decide whether it needs to be cleaned or if it needs a fresh coat of paint. If you have wood-stained trim, it probably needs a good dusting, and then a thorough cleaning with a damp rag or Liquid Gold. I love this stuff. It can bring your tired old woodwork back to life, just be careful not to get it on your walls or carpet, because it is very oily and it could stain!

If your trim is the same color as your walls, then paint it white. White trim offsets the color of the walls, really giving the room a crisp, clean look. Use a high gloss white, for it is very durable and just looks a lot better than flat or satin based finishes.

☐ **A word about wallpaper** – I'm not a fan of wallpaper, especially in a house you're trying to sell. Wallpaper designs are not always exactly neutral and it gives a feeling of permanence, which is not good news if the homebuyer doesn't like it. Okay, so what do you do? I would say take it down and paint a nice earthy color. I'm not looking directly at it though, so this would be a good time to bring in your OP and get an honest opinion. Now, if you get good reviews from your OP, then by all means keep it. Please just try to stay as neutral as you can. I will say that if you have any wallpaper borders, then those *must* come down, no exceptions.

WINDOWS AND DOORS

☐ **Window treatments** - If you have sheets draped over your windows, take them down! Now!

The type of window treatment that you put up will largely depend on the type of window you have. Always remember, neutral, neutral, neutral! No funky colors here. We want whites, beiges, tans, browns, etc. There are plenty of books and magazines that will show you some great and elegant ways to dress your windows if you are confused about what to do. You can never go wrong with two-inch faux wood blinds in white or natural wood, and tab curtains in a neutral beige color. This arrangement will go with just about any type of window in any room in your house. Another no-fail design idea for your windows are white sheer curtains on a café rod or tension rod. The more panels the better, so you get a full blousy look.

Hint: Hang your curtains as high as you can to give added height to your ceilings. Also, try hanging your paneled curtains outside the frame of your window to give the illusion of a bigger window.

☐ **Let the sunshine in!** – Open up those blinds and drapes, and let the sunshine in! When you let light in, it allows the room to appear bigger and that is a definite plus to the homebuyer! Closed blinds can emit a dreary dungeon feeling and can leave you feeling kind of depressed. That is not what we want the homebuyers to feel like, so open it up and let the natural sunlight through.

☐ **Clean those windows!** – Okay, you've dressed up your windows with new treatments and the blinds are open to let the sun shine through. Great! However, if your windows are filthy and that sun shines through, it's not going to be pretty! Let those fresh new window treatments really shine with some beautifully cleaned windows! Inside and out has to be done, and you will be so happy you did. Let's face it; this is the best facelift for your home at a bargain price!

☐ **Sliding Glass Doors** – The first thing we need to address if you have sliding glass doors is that they function properly. Make sure they slide effortlessly and your screen door as well.

Next, we want to look at how your slider is dressed. If you

have vertical blinds on your sliding glass doors or any window in your home, then take them down now! Please! These were great options at one time, very trendy and very dated. Sorry, I don't mean to hurt anyone's feelings (I've had them, too), but these can actually detract from your windows.

I want to suggest that you dress your slider like you would the other windows in your home. In my home I have a double curtain rod with two panels of white shears on the inside and one heavier panel in sage green on either side of the frame. This can make your sliding glass door look a little classier and almost as though it was a large window. Don't forget to clean these when you clean your windows.

☐ **Entry doors (color and hardware)** - A fresh coat of paint in a new or existing color on any of your entry doors could be just what the doctor ordered, especially on your front door. A striking entrance leaves a lasting impression, just make sure it's tasteful. Consider a rich color for your front entrance or a color that will compliment the color of your house and your shutters. If you have a nice wood door, consider refinishing it rather than painting it. If you're in a quandary about what color or stain to choose, talk to the paint professionals at your local home improvement store for some ideas. Don't forget to paint both sides of your doors!

Another way to dress up those outside doors leading in is with new hardware. There are so many different styles and finishes to choose from that you may have a hard time choosing. My personal favorite is the oiled bronze finish in a barn style doorknob. This is currently on our front door and I love it!

I'm a big fan of spray paint, as you know. However, I don't recommend using it on your existing doorknobs, for it will wear and peel real fast due to frequent use.

☐ **Doorknobs and doorstops** - Ask yourself these questions: Are all the doorknobs in the house in working order? Need to be tightened? Do you have a few loose doorknobs that you've been meaning to get to, but don't remember until you go to use that particular door? Are your doorstops (the springy thing on the wall to stop the door) in need of repair? Are you missing doorstops? If you answer yes to any of these questions, then it's time to get to work on these things and repair or replace, whatever is needed.

BEDROOMS

☐ **Bedroom colors** - Like I said before, those neutral shades will work in any room in your house and the bedroom is no exception. Many homebuyers will turn their nose up at a house if they do not like the colors on the walls, and so many of them don't want to put any effort into repainting.

Our oldest son, Steven, is a huge fan of the New York Giants; he has two walls painted red and two walls painted blue. We decorated his room to reflect his personality and it looks great for a teenager. However, when the time comes to sell our house, those wall colors are history.

*Since I started writing this book we have put our house on the market and the New York Giants won the Super Bowl! However, the house being up for sale won out and now Steven's room is a perfectly neutral Cookie Crumb by Glidden!

☐ **Toys** - Don't just throw them in the closet; potential homebuyers will be looking in there as well. This is the time to organize the kids' rooms. Trunks, storage bins, and baskets with lids are a great way to hide some of those toys. If toys are scattered about your house, it's time to make a change. Homebuyers want to see what the rooms' original intention was. If your child's playroom is in the dining room or takes up half of the living room, it takes away from what the room was meant to be and quite simply, it looks bad. Toys belong in the kids' rooms or in a designated playroom, not the dining room!

Pare down by going through some of those old toys the kids do not play with anymore and toss them in your yard sale!

☐ **Beds** - Are your bed linens in good condition, and does the color reflect the neutral palette on your walls, or at least coordinate with it? If not, make sure that it does. Check your magazines for some good ideas, give yourself a budget and be creative.

Do you know how to make a bed? I mean really know how, not just throwing the top sheet or coverlet up over the bed pillows. If you are challenged in this area, I have an easy solution in bed making 101. I want you to go to the mall! Yes, let's go window-shopping at the larger department stores and check out their bed linens and comforters. Now, we're not necessarily going to shop here, but we are going to get some ideas on how to make a bed. These stores always have at least two to three beds made with the linens they sell. Look at how the comforter is turned down, the type of bed skirt used, the sheets, the shams, how they're placed and how many bed pillows and throw pillows are used and grouped. By all means, take notes!

Now, take your newfound information and apply it to your own beds in your home. You can find some great bargains in bedding at your larger 'everything' stores to mimic the more expensive designs. Just remember to keep the palette neutral.

Do you have headboards for the beds in your home? If not, then you need to get some. Headboards seem to anchor the bed in the room and give it some added dimension. A headboard and footboard also makes your bed appear like an actual piece of furniture rather than a pile of linens. I know what you're thinking, and no, you don't have to spend a lot of money. Take a trip to your local thrift store and see what you can find. I bet you'll find something that will work perfect in your space, and always keep in mind that you can customize your new headboard with a little spray paint!

BATHROOMS

☐ **Clean and De-clutter** - First and foremost, you'll want to keep your bathroom clean and clutter free at all times. Put all styling products, blow dryers, curling irons, razors etc., away and off the countertop. A few clutter resolutions could be a basket of hand towels rolled up neatly, a soap dispenser instead of a bar of soap, and drawer organizers/dividers to store hairbrushes, makeup, etc.

Make sure you keep your shower/bathtub, toilet and floors clean. I find it far easier to keep my bathrooms clean on a daily basis when I have cleaning products ready and available. I keep window cleaner, toilet bowl cleaner, tub cleanser and rags in a storage bin under the sink in every bathroom. Since it's always right there, I have no excuse not to wipe things down daily.

Hint: Keep the toilet brush stored under the sink or at the very least, tucked out of sight behind the toilet.

☐ **Bathroom colors** – Yes, your bathroom can have style! With the right finishing touches and a neutral palette, you'll have a show-worthy bathroom in no time. Let's start with color: neutral, neutral and neutral again. Most any earth tone will work in your bathrooms, such as gray, shades of tan and brown, and shades of green with tones of gray. However, don't go too dark. Try to stay on the lighter side of the color spectrum when choosing a certain color, and try to keep in mind the colors of the adjoining rooms. The colors you choose should most definitely compliment one another.

☐ **Shower curtain** - Since you have a nice neutral on your walls, then you can have a little fun with your shower curtain. Notice that I said *little*. Nothing cutsie, kiddy, or outlandishly loud. There are some beautiful and very tasteful designs at your larger *everything* stores. You'll want to find something that has your wall color in it or at least very close to it. By doing this, it better ties the bathroom together. Of course you could go with a white or cream-colored shower curtain and that would be just fine, as long as it is an actual curtain and not just the liner.

☐ **Bathroom mirror** - The days of the oversized frameless mirrors are gone and I can honestly say, thank goodness for small miracles! We have taken all our big mirrors down and replaced them with wood framed mirrors quite a bit smaller than their predecessors, but you don't have to go that far. A great solution to downplay those wall mirrors is to frame them in. Depending on how big you want the actual mirror to be depends on the size molding you install. If you do decide to rip out those old mirrors, then I have some great replacement solutions. You can always find a bargain if you look hard enough and sometimes you don't have to look very hard at all.

Hint: Yard sales and thrift stores are a great place to start! My guest bathroom mirror came from a hotel liquidation store for $10. The only thing I had to do was spray paint the frame the same color as the light fixture. It's beautiful!

Your larger *everything* stores and discounted import stores have awesome bargains as well. Ask about display mirrors, for you may get them at a greater discounted price.

☐ **Bathroom fixtures** – I'm talking sinks, toilets, tubs and faucets. My first question to you is, what color are they? If you have a green, yellow or pink toilet or sink, then they have to go. I think you probably knew I was going to say that, but maybe you just needed to see it in black and white. White is what you want, and you can find new toilets and sinks at your larger home improvement stores at very affordable prices. Since these are big items, it's logical to think that they come with big price tags, but that's not the case here, especially since we're buying to sell.

You can easily update your bathroom faucet, too, if yours is a little grungy and outdated. They make all kinds of styles in just about every finish you can imagine.

Hint: Check out the end caps and clearance aisles of your home improvement stores for deep discounts on these items.

I almost forgot to mention your towel bars. You can update these to match the new fixtures in your bathroom with a few coats of spray paint! Check out the wide selection of paints at your local home improvement stores; you're sure to be amazed!

☐ **Bathroom light fixtures** – You can purchase new light fixtures to update your bathroom, or just paint them – *oh, the power of spray paint!* Since there is such a wide selection of paint finishes to choose from, this to me is the most logical solution to bring those outdated fixtures into the present. To complete the project, update those glass globes and light bulbs as well.

Okay, so you lack time and patience, or your light fixture is just too outdated to even devote one minute to. Not a problem. There are so many fixtures to choose from today and a variety of prices to go along with them. Look through your magazines and browse the lighting section at your local home improvement store to see if there is a light fixture that would be perfect in your bathroom.

Hint: The same applies here as it did for faucets; check the end caps for sales. You're sure to find a bargain!

☐ **Flooring** – I'd be willing to bet that most folks don't have carpet in their bathrooms anymore, but if you happen to be one that does, then it's time to bid it farewell. In case you didn't get the memo, carpet in bathrooms is very outdated and not to mention a big turn-off to homebuyers. I've got good news for you; there are many kinds of flooring options available out there. I'm just going to touch on a couple of my favorites that will work great for you and are very wallet friendly.

Ceramic tiles and/or vinyl textured square tiles can be the perfect update for bathroom floors. Since bathrooms usually have a relatively small square footage area, putting in new flooring can be very inexpensive. Depending on the style and type you choose, both can be very affordable and fairly easy to install. Check the flooring professionals at your local home improvement store for installation instructions.

☐ **White towels** – Yes, white towels! Thick fluffy white towels work with any color you paint your bathroom, so it's not worth spending the money trying to match towel colors to your walls. White is neutral, elegant and clean, and works well with anything. Invest in a decent quality thick towel, hand towels and washcloths. Layer them for an elegant display on your towel bar, rolled up in baskets, and draped over the side of your sink. Use these towels for display only. I repeat, for display only! Keep your bath towels that you use on a daily basis stored in a cabinet out of sight.

Hint: Your bigger everything stores, and bed and bath outlet stores, have great prices on fluffy white bath towels, some as low as $2.99 a towel!

☐ **Decorating your bathroom** – Little touches can go a long way, so keep this simple with a piece of framed art, maybe a black and white print in a black frame with white matting. If you have natural light in your bathroom, then you could even add a small plant in a lined wicker basket. No fake flowers please.

Check out your magazines for some more clever ideas on simple decorating ideas for your bath, and try to keep in mind that you want to enhance, not overwhelm.

KITCHENS

Kitchens can make or break the sale of a house, so you really need to pay close attention to details here. The key is to make your kitchen appear as big as possible while providing functionality paired with a sense of coziness. The kitchen is where family and friends gravitate, so we want to make this the place to be. The homebuyers won't be able to resist it!

☐ **Cabinets** - If you have cabinetry that is outdated, let's see what we can do before we consider taking them down and replacing them. You can give your cabinets an incredible facelift with a few coats of the perfect color and a little hard work. Check with the paint professionals at your local home improvement store for complete start-to-finish instructions on painting cabinets.

Now, if your cabinets are in good condition and not outdated, you may be able to get away with just a good cleaning. Wood oil soap works great on wood cabinets, and good old-fashioned soap and water for other types. When you're all done cleaning up your wood cabinets give them a nice shine with some Liquid Gold. This is the ultimate finishing touch and will make your cabinets pop. You can find Liquid Gold at any store where furniture polish is sold.

Often you will notice cabinetry without any hardware, such as knobs and drawer pulls. Consider giving those cabinets an inexpensive facelift by adding some hardware. There are so many styles and finishes to choose from, you're sure to find knobs that work perfect in your kitchen. Now if you already have knobs but they're in need of a second chance on life, then you know what to do - spray paint them! A finish in a tarnished silver or brushed nickel might be just the ticket! The variety of paint that is available to you is unbelievable, so be choosy when selecting the perfect paint for the job.

How do you determine if you need new cabinets? Are they broken and falling down? Installing new cabinets is not a cheap venture, so make real sure you have exhausted other avenues, such as cleaning and/or painting. Another way to avoid new cabinets all together would be to reface your existing ones. This is a process that involves putting new door, drawer fronts and facing on the existing cabinet boxes. This is quite a bit more affordable than completely replacing everything. The cabinet professionals at your local home improvement store can guide you through any one of these processes.

☐ **Countertops** – Step back and let's evaluate the condition of your countertops. Are there gouges, knife marks, fade marks or permanent stains? Are they an outdated color? If you answered yes to any of these questions, then you may want to consider new countertops. There are so many options available to you in just about any material you can imagine. There are countertops made out of butcher block, granite, marble, tile, laminate, concrete and so much more. Since there is a vast price range, check with your local home improvement stores or specialty cabinet shops to see what they have to offer. You may even find some stores have leftover countertops from a previous install at a discounted rate. I've seen granite remnants at unbelievably low prices. Really do your homework here; explore your options, for they are endless.

☐ **Flooring** – I've talked about flooring earlier in the book and what I said there also applies to the floor in your kitchen. You want a hard surfaced floor, such as ceramic tile, wood floors, laminate wood flooring or textured vinyl square tiles. If your kitchen floor is in need of an update, then you may want to consider one of these flooring options I just mentioned. What you choose will obviously depend on your budget for flooring, and if your budget is tight, my solution to you would be the textured vinyl square tiles. They are very affordable and come in a wide range of colors and designs, and are so easy to install. You may even be able to install these tiles right over the existing floor. Check with the flooring department at your local home improvement store for endless options in flooring materials and installation.

☐ **Lighting** – If you still have one of those big fluorescent lights that looks like it belongs in your garage, then it's time to tell it bye-bye. Flush to the ceiling lighting has got to go as well. Pendant lighting is where it's at folks and they are very affordable. The styles and finishes are varying, as are their price tags. If you see something you like and it's a little pricey, don't be discouraged. My husband and I didn't want to pay the heavy price tag on the pendant lighting in the finish that we wanted, so we bought the less expensive ones and spray-painted them. Score! I get very excited when I feel like I marked an item down myself.

Hint: Check out the end caps and clearance aisles for light fixtures on sale. You're sure to find a bargain.

☐ **Sinks and Faucets** – Can yours just use a good cleaning and polishing? They make some great products to clean and shine, and get the stains out. The product you use will be determined by the condition of your sink, the type of stains you have and the kind of sink you have. For example, you would use a rust remover for rust stains, and you would use a cream polish on an acrylic sink. In almost any situation your sink should be cleanable, but if it's not there are very affordable options available to you. My husband and I bought a brand-new, double acrylic sink for under $80, and there were some that were even less expensive than that.

Kitchen faucets should be cleaned and shined up as well. Even though you may have a very functional faucet you may want to update it for an easy and relatively inexpensive facelift. The homebuyer will appreciate your bringing the kitchen sink into the 21st century.

☐ **Appliances** - Clean all of your appliances, inside and out. Take everything out of your refrigerator and freezer and wipe everything down. Add a fresh box of baking soda to your fridge and freezer to keep odors at bay. Clean your oven and stovetop twice if it needs it. For appliances that need a little more than a good scrubbing, get some appliance spray paint and spruce them up! Yes, they make such a thing and it's wonderful stuff! You can even buy stainless steel paint for your appliances now. Follow directions carefully.

Do your kitchen appliances work? If not, then you need to have them repaired or replaced. It's very simple, you cannot sell a house with broken appliances; these include the refrigerator, oven, stovetop, built-in microwave and dishwasher.

☐ **Kitchen counter clutter** – Now that your kitchen has a new lease on life you really need to keep it clean and free of clutter. The goal is for the homebuyer to see the space in the kitchen, not all of your belongings on the countertops. No more dropping all the mail, bills and paperwork on the counters. If the kitchen is the only place for these things, then you need to put them in a drawer or a basket with a lid.

I would keep canisters, and even a bowl of fruit out for display. You may want to include a vase of flowers, too; this gives the kitchen a homey look and feel. Make whatever adjustments needed until you're satisfied. If you are still stumped, pull out those magazines; the ones you've had out from the beginning!

LAMPS AND LIGHTING

☐ **Lamps** - Do you think your lamps look just fine? Before you answer yes, you'll want to be absolutely sure before you cross this category off your checklist. Look through your magazines, ask your OP, and even better, take a stroll through the lamp department at your larger *everything* store or any lighting retail store. If you find that they are outdated, make a few changes without spending a lot of money for new ones. See if a fresh coat of spray paint would perk up the base of the lamp. I know it will, as all of my lamps have been made new with spray paint! You can also find inexpensive lampshades at your larger *everything* stores. Your larger home improvement stores are now carrying a large selection of lampshades in all the current styles, and are very affordable as well.

Hint: Keep it classic with white lampshades.

Don't cross out the thrift stores for this one; I have found many bargain lamps at the local thrift store, taken them home and spruced them up with a little paint! Voila! A new lamp!

☐ **Chandeliers** – If you have a chandelier in your dining area or anywhere else in your home, like the foyer, then you'll want to make sure they are functional and beautiful. I'm looking for updated here, and brass chandeliers are not it. It seems like homebuilders went crazy with brass light fixtures for a while there, and I suppose they were in style.

You can take your tired old, outdated chandelier and make it current with a can of spray paint, in your favorite new finish, and some new globes. If you happen to have a chandelier with those flame light bulbs, consider topping them with mini lampshades. It's a beautiful look and gives your light fixture a great update.

Check the lighting department at your local home improvement store for the latest fashions in chandeliers. Just knowing what the newest styles and finishes are will give you a great place to start.

☐ **Mood lighting** - With everything that you've done to the house to get it ready to sell, we don't want to spoil it with the wrong lighting. I am referring to the wattage in your lamps, sconces, and overhead lighting. For example, lower the wattage in your fixtures - this creates a cozy feeling in the room. For instance, if you have 60-watt bulbs in your lamps, try 40 watts or even 25 watts. Candles also help create a nice mood as well. A combination of candles and subtle lighting will give your house a sense of warmth and coziness.

☐ **Ceiling fans** - If you have the pleasure of having ceiling fans in your home, make sure they are clean. Fans can collect a lot of dust really fast and so does the ceiling that surrounds them. Look to see where your ceiling fans are hung in your home and decide if a regular light fixture would look or function better. One more point: Are they outdated and ugly? I'm sorry to say, but not all fans are created equal. Here's what you can do to bring yours up-to-date and look brand new. You guessed it - *spray paint*! You can spray paint the blades and the fixture itself. Go to your local home improvement store and check out the ceiling fans, really looking at blade and fixture color. Next, go to the paint section and see what your options are in spray paint colors. If your fan has light fixtures as well, these can also be updated. And there you have it, a brand new ceiling fan for next to nothing!

Note: Don't try to paint the fan while it's still hanging. You must take it down and disassemble it first.

RE-DECORATING YOUR SPACE

We're going down the homestretch! This is by far my favorite part of the journey, partly because we're almost done, but mostly because it's fun to bring a room back together. This section will address all those things in your 'keep' pile, and I'll also give hints on how to cozy-up your home and lure those homebuyers in. Let's get started so we can get done!

☐ **Furniture** - Let's take a look at the furniture in your keep piles for each designated room and decide whether it's going to work or not. I'd like you to get your OP to give you an honest assessment to the condition of your sofa and other furniture. This may seem irrelevant to the sale of your house, but we have to keep in mind the eyesight of future homebuyers. If the couch is a little outdated with patterns only you could love or the colors are less than neutral, slipcovers make a wonderful alternative to buying new furniture. You can find slipcovers for just about any chair or sofa at your bigger "everything" stores. They also make them in about every neutral shade and earth tone you could imagine, and remember, no patterns. Another good idea would be to check your local thrift stores. I have seen some nice furniture at thrift stores for next to nothing. Check your magazines and arrange them in an eye-pleasing manner that gives good composition to the room. I'll say it one more time, get your magazines and your OP in on this and have fun!

☐ **Furniture position** - The way you position the furniture in your room will let people see how big or how small the room is, and this goes for every room in your house. The main objective is to make the room appear cozy without making it look small. Ask your OP and look through your magazines carefully. Play around with the position of your furniture, because that is how you're going to find out what works best in the room. You may need to put a few pieces in another room or just store it out in the garage. I really want to encourage you to float some pieces of furniture, like the sofa, in the middle of the room. I know this sounds scary to a lot of people, but try to get your furniture off your walls. I wish I could come into everyone's house and help you out with this, because everyone's room is shaped differently; however, I know you can do it! Remember, less can oftentimes mean more, so be careful not to overcrowd your room with too much furniture or with furniture that is too big. Have fun and play around with it.

If you are completely lost when it comes to pulling your rooms back together, you always have the option of calling in a Home Interior Re-arranger. These people specialize in re-arranging your furniture and other belongings so that they are pleasing to the eye and create composition in the room. They charge by the hour or by the room, and are a lot more reasonable than an interior decorator would be. Check the Internet or phone book for re-arrangers in your area.

☐ **Wall hangings** - Now that you have painted the walls a nice neutral color and your furniture is in position, it's time to put some things back up on the wall and do a little decorating. Sort through that 'keep' pile of pictures and paintings, and decide what stays and what can be packed up. My suggestion is that your artwork be minimal and neutral in color. When staging a home to be sold, black and white artwork works well in the room, as it enhances not overwhelms, allowing the room to take center-stage. Another suggestion would be to keep the frames your artwork is in the same color. I have painted all my frames a rich chocolate brown and it has tied my artwork together and created a sense of continuity. Framed mirrors are another great and easy way to decorate your walls. If you don't have any pictures already and you're on a strict budget, yard sales and thrift stores are a great place to start. "Everything" stores are another option. They have a great selection, and at these stores you'll find pictures that match and coordinate with each other. Regardless of the room, it's important to have some art on your walls.

Hint: when you're ready to hang pictures, group them in odd numbers on your wall. I don't know why it is, but odd numbers are just more pleasing to the eye. So, a single picture or a group of 3 or 5 will do the job. This rule can be applied to every decorating situation you encounter from grouping candleholders on your mantle to grouping framed photographs on a table. Try it and you'll see.

☐ **Decorating fillers** – These are things that will fill in what seems to be missing in the room and make it look complete, lived in and comfortable.

Books – Books are great to own, to display and to decorate with. Of course they work great on a bookshelf, but they also work well as filler on your coffee table or end tables. You'll want to use an oversized hardcover book, or books stacked on one another. The size of your books greatly depends on the size of the table; the smaller the table the smaller your books should be. The content of the book should be taken into consideration as well. I keep a large hardcover book of America's history on our coffee table along with a chunky candle and a small plant. (Remember that odd number rule).

Candles – I love candles and I feel as though they emit a sense of soothing warmth. Check with your OP and your magazines for placement of your candles. You will also want to take a good look at your candleholders to make sure they are similar in style to one another and that they look good. My suggestion is no brass, weird-style candleholders or glass jar candles. If brass is all you have, then grab some spray paint or take a trip to the store and hunt for some new ones. You will also want to use white or beige candles only. We are keeping up with the simplistic theme here, so no colored candles.

Aromas - Make sure that your house always smells good. There are so many scents to choose from. Harvest scents, such as apple, cinnamon and vanilla, are some of my favorites. The goal is to have potential homebuyers feel that they are entering a cozy, warm house. This can be accomplished by using scented plug-in room deodorizers, sachets, scented candles or cinnamon scented pinecones in a basket. Find the one that works for you. Another great way to pour on the smell is to simmer some cinnamon sticks with a little dash of nutmeg and cloves on the stove before an open house. Yum! It'll smell great and your guests will feel at home.

Plants – Plants are a great way to add a feeling of warmth to your home. However, you don't want a jungle! There is such a thing as too much, and if you have too many plants for the size space you have, then give some away or loan them out while your house is up for sale.

Make sure your plant containers are in good shape and not in a multitude of colors. Continue the theme of continuity and keep those containers relatively close to the same. No plastic containers.

Fireplace and Mantel - A fireplace is a wonderful asset to your home and most homebuyers would agree. To really show it off and make it stand out, I would suggest you have a fire going in it at the time your house is being shown. Of course you'll want to make sure your fireplace is functional and clean. The hearth should be clean as well as the chimney. If necessary, have your chimney professionally cleaned.

Now, you know you have to decorate that mantle. Check your magazines for good composition, color and ideas on how to stage your mantle. You may be surprised at the different items that you can use to decorate the mantle with. Keep in mind the odd number rule and have fun.

MISCELLANEOUS INSIDE

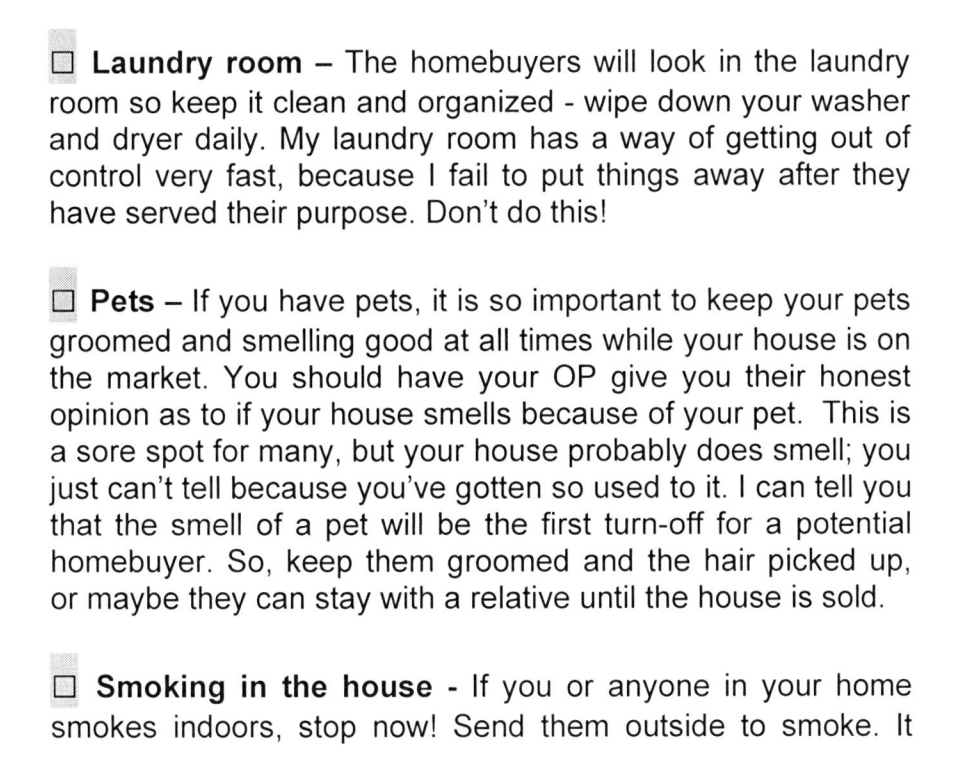

☐ **Laundry room** – The homebuyers will look in the laundry room so keep it clean and organized - wipe down your washer and dryer daily. My laundry room has a way of getting out of control very fast, because I fail to put things away after they have served their purpose. Don't do this!

☐ **Pets** – If you have pets, it is so important to keep your pets groomed and smelling good at all times while your house is on the market. You should have your OP give you their honest opinion as to if your house smells because of your pet. This is a sore spot for many, but your house probably does smell; you just can't tell because you've gotten so used to it. I can tell you that the smell of a pet will be the first turn-off for a potential homebuyer. So, keep them groomed and the hair picked up, or maybe they can stay with a relative until the house is sold.

☐ **Smoking in the house** - If you or anyone in your home smokes indoors, stop now! Send them outside to smoke. It doesn't matter how much smelly stuff you spray in the air, people can still smell the smoke. It permeates everything that is in your home, from your furniture to your drapes, and so on. You've gone to a lot of trouble to get your house in awesome shape, so why go and blow it by smoking in the house? You could potentially blow a sale, too. Think about it.

KEEP IT CLEAN

When your house is on the market you never know when a homebuyer will want to come by and take a look. On that note, you'll want to keep your house clean and tidy at all times.

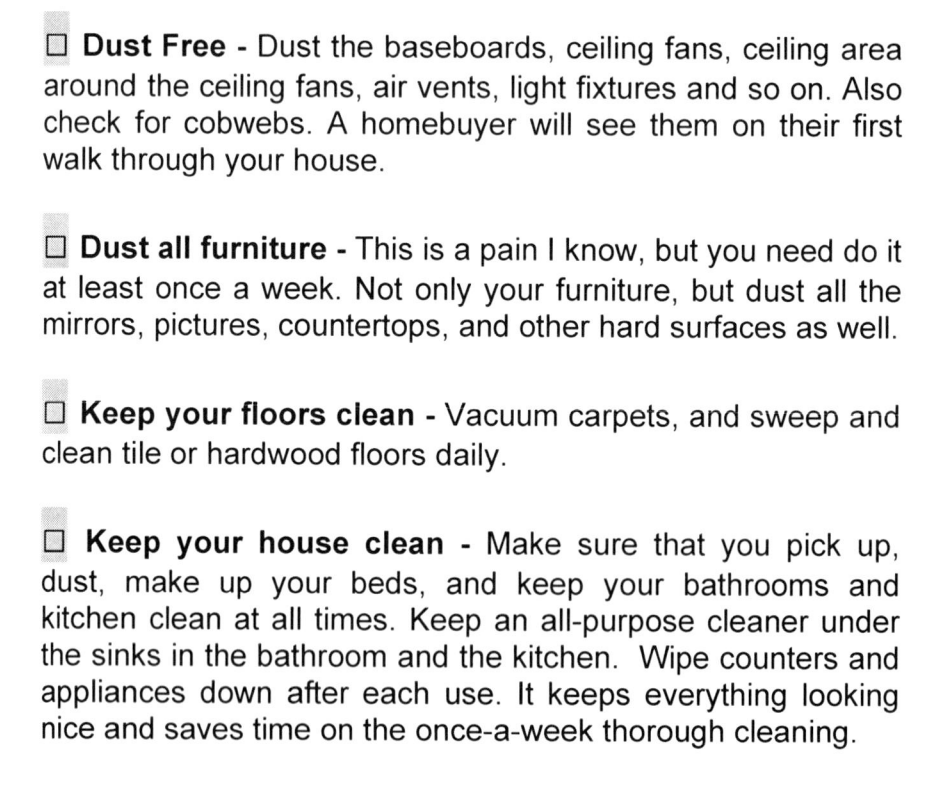

☐ **Dust Free** - Dust the baseboards, ceiling fans, ceiling area around the ceiling fans, air vents, light fixtures and so on. Also check for cobwebs. A homebuyer will see them on their first walk through your house.

☐ **Dust all furniture** - This is a pain I know, but you need do it at least once a week. Not only your furniture, but dust all the mirrors, pictures, countertops, and other hard surfaces as well.

☐ **Keep your floors clean** - Vacuum carpets, and sweep and clean tile or hardwood floors daily.

☐ **Keep your house clean** - Make sure that you pick up, dust, make up your beds, and keep your bathrooms and kitchen clean at all times. Keep an all-purpose cleaner under the sinks in the bathroom and the kitchen. Wipe counters and appliances down after each use. It keeps everything looking nice and saves time on the once-a-week thorough cleaning.

There you have it! I've given you over 100 different things to look at in and around your home. I hope you've learned that selling your house involves more than just handing the keys over to a realtor. You are an integral part of the process and responsible for the quality of the merchandise sold, which is your home. Hopefully, it wasn't too overwhelming for you and I trust you were able to get to everything that required special attention. Along the way you may have come across some tasks I didn't mention and if you did, I would love to hear from you. I may even include any new ideas in my next book.

Here's my contact information: **sell-your-house@hotmail.com**

Good luck selling your house and best wishes settling into your new home!